W9-AOX-775

ALBERT PUJOLS

Joe Gaspar

PowerKiDS press.

New York

Published in 2011 by The Rosen Publishing Group, Inc.
29 East 21st Street, New York, NY 10010

First Edition

Editor: Amelie von Zumbusch
Book Design: Kate Laczynski
Photo Researcher: Jessica Gerweck

Photo Credits: Cover, pp. 1, 7 Stephen Dunn/Wire Image/Getty
Images; p. 4 Leon Halip/Getty Images; p. 8 Allen Kee/Wire Image/
Getty Images; p. 11 Doug Pensinger/Getty Images; p. 12 Scott
Boehm/Getty Images; pp. 15, 16 Dilip Vishwanat/Stringer/Getty
Images; pp. 19, 22 Jed Jacobsohn/Getty Images; p. 20 Associated
Press/AP Images.

Library of Congress Cataloging-in-Publication Data

Gaspar, Joe.
  Albert Pujols / Joe Gaspar.
    p. cm.
  Includes index.
  ISBN 978-1-4488-0629-4 (library binding) —
ISBN 978-1-4488-1782-5 (pbk.) — ISBN 978-1-4488-1783-2
(6-pack)
  1. Pujols, Albert, 1980—Juvenile literature. 2. Baseball players—
Dominican Republic—Biography—Juvenile literature. I. Title.
  GV865.P85G37 2011
  796.357092—dc22
  [B]
                    2009045163

Manufactured in the United States of America

CPSIA Compliance Information: Batch #WS10PK: For Further Information contact Rosen Publishing, New York, New York at
1-800-237-9932

CONTENTS

4

Albert Pujols is a great baseball player. He was born in the Dominican Republic.

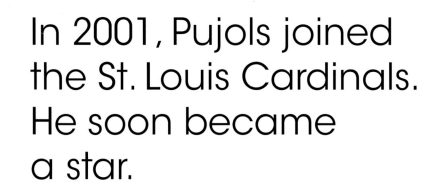

In 2001, Pujols joined the St. Louis Cardinals. He soon became a star.

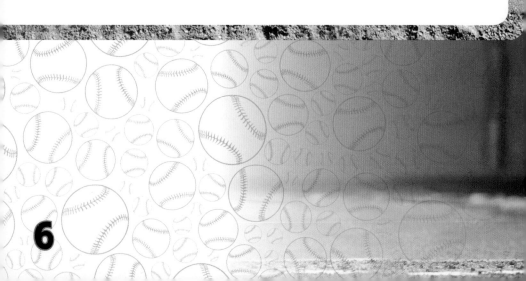

Pujols hit a home run in his first game! He hits lots of home runs.

Pujols is a great hitter. He has won **awards** for his hitting.

11

He is good at running the bases, too. Pujols runs fast!

Pujols plays first base.
He is one of today's
best first basemen.

15

Pujols gets along well with his **teammates**.

In 2006, Pujols helped the Cardinals win the **World Series**.

19

20

Pujols was named the MVP, or most **valuable** player, in 2005, 2008, and 2009.

Albert Pujols loves baseball. He is a great player.

BOOKS

Here are more books to read about Albert Pujols and baseball:

Kelley, K. C. *St. Louis Cardinals.* Favorite Baseball
　　Teams. Mankato, MN: The Child's World, Inc., 2010.

Mattern, Joanne. *Albert Pujols.* Robbie Readers.
　　Hockessin, DE: Mitchell Lane Publishers, Inc., 2007.

WEB SITES

Due to the changing nature of Internet links,
PowerKids Press has developed an online list of
Web sites related to the subject of this book. This
site is updated regularly. Please use this link to
access the list:
www.powerkidslinks.com/bmvp/ap/

GLOSSARY

awards (uh-WORDZ) Special honors given to people.

teammates (TEEM-mayts) People who play for the same team.

valuable (VAL-yoo-bul) Important.

World Series (WURLD SEER-eez) A group of games in which the two best baseball teams play against each other.

INDEX